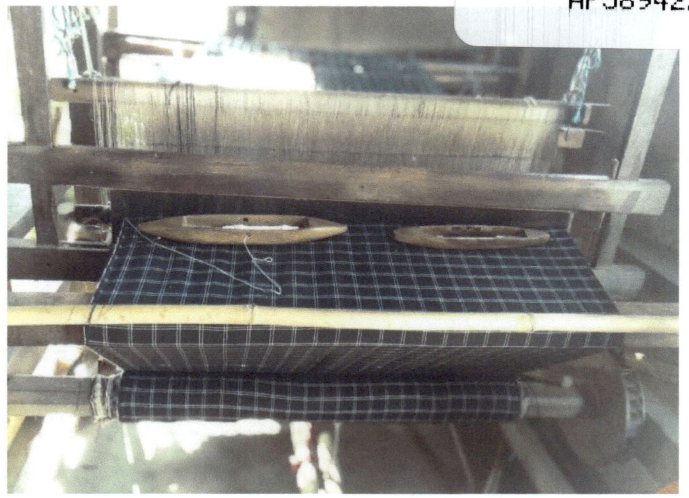

PANGABLAN

The Living Treasure of Paoay

By

Jenifer Caracar-Macadangdang

by Jenifer Caracar-Macadangdang

ISBN:
Softbound- 978-621-8261-50-1
Hardbound- 978-621-8261-51-8
Mobile/kindle- 978-621-8261-52-5

Published by Poetry Planet Book Publishing House
Cover photo by: Alexandria Eigram G. Eclarin
Edited Marie Ezekiel
Photos by:
Mark Angelo Damo
Christopher Calapini Abuy
Mark-Alvin Bautista Caracar
Jonalyn Niog Libed
Jenifer Caracar-Macadangdang

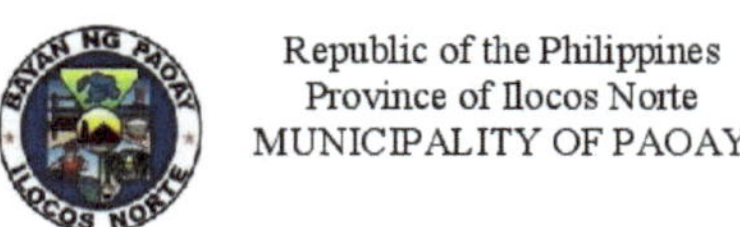

Republic of the Philippines
Province of Ilocos Norte
MUNICIPALITY OF PAOAY

OFFICE OF THE MAYOR

FOREWORD

The Municipality of Paoay has undeniably kept a glorious history as traditions, tangible and intangible, are still being practiced and customs observed. Abel-weaving is one of the few surviving traditional crafts in Paoay. On the whole, it follows a very intricate process – from preparing and dyeing the yarn, to arranging different colors of yarn to produce the desired design, and operating the wooden handloom with the synchronized movement of both hands and feet.

Today, the abel is no longer just an indigenous Ilocano fabric known for its sturdy and versatile quality. With over two centuries of history behind it have metamorphosed from the traditional blankets and bed covers, pillow cases, mosquito nets, bath towels and robes, hand towels, place mats and table napkins, runners, and hand towels to become a modern day apparel, as it has become the fabric of choice of a lot of designers.

However, we have seen the dwindling lack of interest of the younger generation. With the technological advancements today, their activities are now mostly focused on online platforms and their interests have changed. Hence, there is a need to give a boost to the abel industry so that it could survive the vicissitudes of time

"PANGABLAN: The Living Treasure of Paoay," is a tapestry of culture–infused essays that preserves the sounds, scents and splendors of the humble loom, a cultural symbol that stood witness to every Paoayeños beautifully woven life. This book is truly a masterpiece that would remind everyone the values of perseverance, love, hardwork, determination and passion. Further, it bespeaks of our resiliency as a people.

On behalf of the Local Government Unit of Paoay, Ilocos Norte, I extend my warmest commendation to Ms. Jenifer Caracar-Macadangdang for her notable accomplishment. I hope that this beautiful work shall inspire the youth to venture into this wonderful Ilocano art. We can bet that if abel-weaving is given back its splendour, with the resiliency of the Paoayeño, it will continue to weave a history that would become another great ilocano epic.

ROMULO L. ACDAL, JR. MD
Acting Municipal Mayor

DEDICATION

This humble accomplishment is dedicated to the following sources of inspiration. Without them, this dream would not be a reality...

To the greatest weaver I've known and the greatest mother I had, my *Nanang* Ofelia Bautista Caracar;

To my loving and supportive husband Rufino, and my sweet daughters Kyle Zyrah and Anna Carmella;

To my brothers and sisters, friends and relatives;

To my beloved municipality of Paoay, Ilocos Norte; and

To God Almighty, the source of my writing prowess and confidence.

-The Author

PREFACE

"A mother's love is the fuel that enables a normal human being to do the impossible." - Marion C. Garretty.

There is no greater love than a mother's love. It is unconditional and beyond compare. Our mothers are the most consistent person who would motivate us to be the best version of ourselves.

I, myself, had experienced that purest kind of love. It was imprinted in my heart and had ignited my desire to really do the things I thought were impossible for me to accomplish. Yes, I never thought of becoming a book author. However, my mother's investment of love in me had resulted in this brainchild, this humble book of our hardships, struggles, memories, and victories.

This book is not only memorabilia of a great weaver and a great mother but also a reflection of my beloved municipality's rich and unique cultural heritage- its scents, sights, and splendors!

This anthology of feature articles showcases the beauty and grandeur of Paoay, Ilocos Norte while reflecting our desirable values as Ilocanos. From the golden sands of the dunes of Paoay to the majestic architectural design of the Paoay Church, a UNESCO World Heritage Site, our stories were scribbled to form a versatile tapestry which is the Pangablan: The Living Treasure of Paoay.

This book is a labor of love and a gift to the next generations to come.

Jenifer Caracar-Macadangdang
Author

TABLE OF CONTENTS

CHAPTER 1

PANGABLAN

THE WEAVER OF OUR FUTURE

She was so fine as the thread and so strong as the loom...

Whenever I come across a story of success from others who struggled a lot, I always find myself marveling among the characters. One of which certainly would make it to the list was the story of my mother Ofelia Bautista Caracar.

As Shakespeare once said that all the world's a stage, and all the men and women merely players; they have their exits and their entrances, and one man in his time plays many parts, my

mother had her entrance into this beautiful yet challenging world on March 7, 1955. She was the third fruit of love of Anterio Sutsut Bautista and Pacita Lumang Bautista. She was trained to be a prolific artist and to be a person of desirable values.

At the early age of 17, my mother found her soulmate when he married my father Simplicio Galano Caracar, a fisherman and at the same time a bus conductor from Nagbacalan, Paoay, Ilocos Norte. They were blessed with 5 children.

We lived a simple yet happy life and shared wonderful memories together. We weaved abel and our dreams together. However, it was then April 23, 1999, when my father bid goodbye to earthly life and left everything under my mother's supervision and responsibility. I still vividly remember my parents' powerful lines that served as the most inspiring script of my play- *Agadalka a nasayaat anakko tapno magun-odmo dagiti arapaapmo. Kas ti panagabel, abelem ti arapaapmo babaen ti anus, gaget ken kinasayaat iti padam a tao* (Study hard my child so that you'll be able to achieve your dreams.

Like weaving, weave your dreams through perseverance, hard work, and kindness to others).

At 66 years old, we, her five children were now degree holders. And it is all because of her constant reminders and unconditional love and care to us. She was not able to pursue a bachelor's degree, however, her level of expertise when it comes to weaving was so immense and distinguished that if you would take a look at her crafts and designs, you would definitely doubt her eligibility claiming that she only attained elementary level. Her expertise in her field of *panagabel* (weaving) is truly exemplary. Her beautiful tapestries reminded us of how beautiful life is. They reminded us that like them we follow patterns that would bring out the best in us.

My eldest sister Jannet Caracar Villorente was a graduate of computer secretarial. She was married to Cleody Villorente, and now a mother of three children named Fredrick, Patrick, and Trisha. Their family now lives at Iba Zambales. Though not weaving *abel* there anymore, the life lessons we learned from our mother run in her children's blood.

I, the second child, Jenifer Caracar Macadangdang, is now a Public School teacher at Nagbacalan Elementary School, Paoay District, Paoay Ilocos Norte. I was married to Rufino Macadangdang, Jr., and was blessed with two children named Kyle Zyrah and Ana Carmella. I wrote this humble book as dedication and a tribute to my loving mother.

The third child, Rackie Bautista Caracar, my younger brother, obtained the degree Bachelor of Science in Industrial Technology. Rackie works as Chief Cook at Maersk Filipinas Crewing Inc. He was married to Jonna Erni Caracar in which they now have two offspring named Fiona Beatrizze and Schuyler Arkin and happily living in Cavite.

The fourth child Catherine Caracar Daquiaog, my younger sister attained college level and is now a Domestic helper in Hongkong. Catherine was married to Joey Daquiaog and they were blessed with two children named Karl Yeoj and Chrystene Faye.

Meanwhile, our youngest sibling Mark Alvin Bautista Caracar obtained a degree in Bachelor of Science in Industrial Technology, major in Electronics. Mark Alvin is still a bachelor but he already works as Officer-In-Charge at Paoay Faith Academy, Paoay, Ilocos Norte.

We really have different paths to take; however, whatever life has for us, will and determination should be lit fiery within our spirits.

Just like this humble loom weaver, our mother Ofelia Caracar Bautista, who would have thought that she could make it this great?

It may have had cost her life in sacrifice for our welfare --- for the dreams we had aspired--- this however does not undermine her strength nor sank her courage, because whatever she did, it is for the fulfillment of her promises not only as our mother but also as a loving wife to our deceased father.

Indeed, her exit in the stage of life was graceful enough because she was able to finish her masterpiece--- the tapestry of our lives. The values we learned from her will forever be imprinted in our hearts. She is indeed one of the greatest weavers of the future we have ever met and known.

THE LOOM

In the Ilocos Region, the *Inabel/abel iloko* or woven fabric is one of the well-known products. The loom is considered the soul of the municipality of Paoay because it is where the most woven cloth and tapestry came from.

When I was young, I used to watch elders around us on how they weave. The rhythm of their hands and feet was so amusing. They're like playing as they weave blankets, towels, curtains,

table runners, and many more merchandise from the loom.

My father Simplicio Galano Caracar is a fisherman. Meanwhile, my mother Ofelia Bautista Caracar is simply a usual housewife. We're five, three were girls, and two were boys. Despite the struggle that surfaces, our parents aspire that we could one day hold degrees.

Our father always reminds us that: "If there's perseverance, there's food." He's so hardworking. But because of his unstable source of income, we often had a scarcity of necessities every day.

"Let's twofold our perseverance succeed," our mother insinuates. She's very productive and always desires to find ways in helping our father.

I once caught our parents having a conversation on how they will they send us to school. And I heard that our mother pleas to own a loom at least. Weaving really pleases her. That's perhaps the reason why she always yearns to learn how to weave on our neighbors. When she learned it, they've made it possible to commission their own loom. The truth is, they just borrowed their investment to begin, especially those spent on purchasing materials and many others.

The cotton thread before was white. It still needs to be dyed to reproduce another shade. This made it an arduous task in weaving. However, a decade after, colorful cotton thread was available in the marketplace. It made the magnificent evolution of designs within the merchandise of *abel Iloko.*

Our mother was so ecstatic when she started weaving with her loom. After her household tasks, she would master the weaving. I once heard our mother says, "This loom won't just weave fabrics, because it would also especially weave our dreams."

She seems tireless. None of her time is wasted for she always weaves. She would often instantaneously sing as she starts weaving. Sometimes, there's a radio transistor on her side. We would accompany her silently while listening for she doesn't want to be disturbed when she has something to weave.

I'll hum our youngest one to sleep, then proceed in picking grasses around the house to assist our mother. There's a cradle near the loom. Our youngest usually fall deep into sleep whenever he knew that our mother lays next to her, especially whenever he hears the tickling sound the weaving machine creates while our mother sits with it.

Due to the uncontrollable number of customers especially those businessmen who ordered my mother's finished product, she became more active in weaving. She even made her own design. Then, as time goes by, the beauty in her works has seen and became more attractive.

There was a time that a lot of customers ordered blankets. Our mother needed to travel to Cagayan, Isabela, and Apayao. She didn't make it up to go home early for she vigorously sells those weave cloths. Despite having no electricity back then, she still patiently proceeded with a gas lamp hanged.

"You've had enough my dear, you better stop, or else it might ruin your eyesight," my father muttered.

"What's important dear is that our children's dreams won't be ruined. Our sacrifices were for them."

There was a time, my father turned off the gas lamp to where mother is. She had no choice but to stop weaving. The night was filled with silence and we all quietly sleep as the loom is.

One day, I was awakened from my sleep. My parents were happily having their conversation near the weaving machine while slurping their coffee. I've heard them saying that one day we could be able to pursue our dreams. I am not the only witness of what transpired that day, but also the loom that is just waiting to be used.

IDIOSYNCRATIC ABEL OF PAOAY

If you work with your own hands, the quality is higher, that is the difference of our Abel in the commercial market. - Charito Carraiga.

Pangablan Products are the finest, known for its durability, softness, and uniqueness. I have featured few although there are numerous creations that are used daily and comfortably by common people. I know because I am the living witness how Loom weaving and its products became part of my daily life, such creativity that turns into a legacy, something we are proud of sharing to our future generations…

BLANKET: As Warm As Mother's Love

Blankets are what my mother Ofelia mostly weaves. Buyers usually are in awe of her merchandise because the color combinations of cotton threads used were so cool that it soothes the eye. Moreover, her works seem to reflect the signature of tribal designs. She could knit the names of the buyers into her designs up until personalized blanket becomes the trend.

All our blankets in our home were *abel-iloko* made. What I really love about this kind of blanket

is that it does not easily smell foul whenever used, so light to wash and easy to dry.

Our parents usually wrap blankets as wedding gifts whenever there's one. Mother typically knit patiently the names of the groom and bride as part of the design. What a lasting and fine remembrance it is they say whenever a blanket was given.

I could vividly remember that when I was young, I cannot sleep well and sound if I were to use another blanket. My body constantly seeks the *abel-Iloko* blanket that I initially used. "Gosh, you're just attached to what you smell like," father said. They once took my blanket to the laundry and it did not dry quickly. I couldn't sleep that night. Mother noticed that I was crying. She shielded me from my father's attempt to reprimand. "He's actually looking for the blanket that usually covers him throughout the night. That blanket seems to have a life in giving him warmth."

There's a day where father had no catch and we don't have any viand to eat. He is worried because it's getting dark. Mother went out. And didn't say a thing. About roughly ten minutes, she came back. She had her along with some vegetables for Pinakbet and a half-kilo of meat to mix with. She sweetly smiled as she put down these on our table.

"Where did you get some money to buy?" father asked as he was staring at her.

"I sold one of the blankets that were ordered by our relatives in Cagayan," mother retorted. "Don't worry, I'll quickly make some soon and bring it to them," she added.

That's how diligent our mother Ofelia is. She seems to be inexhaustible. You won't hear her complaining though sometimes, her face cannot anymore hide how tired she is.

"Please do rest, dear. You're exploiting yourself," father worriedly reminded her.

"No, I am not that tired. Weaving for me is nothing but only a common exercise. It's more tiring I think If I just lay still," mother stressed.

There was once an incident where my two siblings fell ill. They went to the folk healer but they didn't get well. It was because they're hesitating to have them admit to the hospital due to insufficient savings for medical expenses. However, Mother insists to bring them there. As they approached the hospital, father stayed. Meanwhile, mother went out to find some money. The truth is, she sold every blanket that she had kept which is supposedly intended only for trading rice.

"Don't you feel at loss selling your blankets at less than minimum?" father desolately whispered. It is because he already knew how cheap the price is when wholesaled to neighbors who also trade woven merchandise.

"I won't mind feeling at loss in selling those blankets that were hardly produced as long as it is for the welfare of our family and for the aspirations it has. I firmly trust that our God would soon fill what was lost," she answered with a sweetened smile. And I saw how they tightly embraced each one.

When my siblings just came home from the hospital, I couldn't really forget what Mother told us. "For as long as this loom stays with us, hope won't fade away." Our mother Ofelia unceasingly smiled as she sips her coffee.

THE BODY TOWEL REVEALS A SECRET

One best feature perhaps our mother Ofelia has that we love so much is her attentive and thoughtful nature. Not only she is a loving spouse but also a responsible mother to her five kids. That's the reason why we dearly love our mother. She may not be a perfect one but she lacks none as the light of our humble home.

I could still vibrantly remember when I was about 12 years old, our father's body towel

suddenly disappears. He was really extremely in despair because that was a gift from his parents back then when he was still a bachelor.

"Forget it, dear, that was already so old too. Time for a change," mother cheered.

"That body towel has so many memories in it. It is so sentimental to me," father sadly mumbled.

"I'll just make one for you similar to what was lost," mother vowed.

Just when Father left to fish, she went straight to the loom. I already knew she would make a body towel for our father to fulfill what was promised.

It was almost eve when mother started preparing father's clothes. That was his usual time to take a bath. Mother showed the woven body towel made for him.

"You are undoubtedly master of your craft, dear, the texture and design were perfect. This is very similar to my lost body towel," our father Simplicio exclaimed in tears.

She just smiled. Her eyes were pleased while watching father embrace his new body towel.

However, I was really surprised by what I just discovered one day. I saw father's former body towel lying on the ground while flames slowly devour its entirety. I have seen it when I went to throw some trash.

I told mother what I saw. We made a promise not to tell anyone regarding the burning body towel. She really planned to burn the body towel because it was so old and it has already two fist-like holes in it.

The former body towel is indisputably fragile and old. However, whenever I see my father's new body towel, I can't help but smile. Mother do really love our father.

THE FACE TOWEL'S LOVE SPELL

According to size, face towel is the smallest of all *abel-iloko*. If there's an extra thread, our mother Ofelia would weave these into face towels so as not to waste excesses.

They often tell us that face towel is the reason why fate brought them together. This was their story: They're both passengers and coincidentally seated next to each one on a bus heading from Cagayan to Ilocos Norte. In the middle of their travel, mother felt thirsty. When

she's about to drink, water tripped unto her face when the bus driver suddenly took a break. Our father quickly grabbed the face towel buried in his pocket then lent it to our mother which she used to wipe her face. That's where it started. They've exchanged conversations. Till father courted her then sealed their marriage.

We heard such a story once at a usual family dinner. Actually, that face towel that was once witnessed to their unexpected love story, was still kept and hidden until now. My father then was an employee of Chona Patrick Liner that bound Cagayan to Ilocos Norte

Mother already weaved many face towels. It comes in different sizes based on the preferences of customers. This is such a nice thing to wrap as a gift because not only it is lovely, but it could also be at affordable prices.

"Father's face towel contains magic spell, isn't it, mother? What a lucky face towel it is," I once teasingly said.

"It is your father's heart none other contain that magic spell…and I believe so that I am more fortunate than that face towel," mother expressed while laughing.

Whenever mother weaves face towels, she would silently whisper that hopefully this won't be just used to rub dirt, tears, and colds.

I wish, however, that every face towel could make a lovely story of life to whosoever owns it.

When I was in sophomore high school, I found a pair of face towels on the ground near the gate. Both towels have embroidered names on them. The face towels belong to a rich family. The owner rewarded me cash upon returning to them for those small things had sentimental value for them. What a joy in my heart! The handkerchief-sized towels became an instrument for me to buy a necessary project on that grading period.

THE PILLOWCASE AND A LOVE STORY

Among all the woven cloth that my mother made, the pillowcase is their most preferred. This perhaps because each was paired that is suited for couples or those who live under the same roof. Most of them were fond of this *Abel-Iloko* because it was made of cotton and it gratifies the skin. Many make orders from Cagayan, then across Isabela and even abroad.

The pillowcase of our father and mother was already old --- knitted with the name Caracar~Bautista. They're not getting a new one, for they believed that the pillowcase had strengthened their love for each other.

There was a time when mother had to sell *Abel-Iloko* merchandise in Cagayan particularly in the town of Pamplona where she was raised. She traded her product with rice, especially glutinous rice.

But every time my mother travels, she used to take my father's pillowcase secretly. She really can't sleep without leaning on it, according to her.

One time, my father got irritated. As our mother arrived, he told her that she should make another pair. "Did you know that I also can't sleep without you, and I was really hoping that at least even just your smell stays on it?", father whined.

Mother then weaved one. She knitted names on their pillowcase with Ofelia~Simplicio. Meanwhile, she gave it to Father.

"Did you know that it doesn't feel well having separated pillowcases? It feels like one of us might disappear if they were not conjoined", Father clearly explained.

When I got married, I ordered three pairs of personalized pillowcases. It is indeed true, that whenever my wife wasn't beside me, it is sufficient to embrace a pillow where I could see her name knitted on it.

I know most of us *Paoayeños* have our pillowcases. We personally patronize our products by using them most often. Whenever we have visitors, pillowcases are always ready for them to use.

THE MAJESTIC TABLE CLOTH

Buyers purchase table cloth rarely. Our mother Ofelia doesn't like to have a stock of this product due to varying sizes of tables from those buyers. But if there's someone who wants to have such, mother would still weave for them as she loves to sit with the loom.

My mother is so excellent at designing table clothes. There are some churches where she made table cloth for them. Some restaurants have their design made by her. That is the reason why I said that my mom is so talented. I salute her expertise in weaving.

There's a story behind the tablecloth in our home. Inside our parent's room, we seldom go there because they do not want those fabrics or decorations to neither be touched nor moved. Way back when we were little, it is true that we're too playful.

There was a time that I noticed my father put a paper below the table cloth in their room. To my interest, I secretly picked what is in there. It was a letter of apology.

I read it. I was surprised. The content goes like this, "Sorry, dear, if there is anything I've said that offended you. I just wanted to tell you that I was only teasing you. I love you. I've had no other Ofelia in my life for no other else than you."

I have never seen our parents had their fights when it comes to affection. If there's any, it is because they are quiet. I didn't tell anyone about the letter. I needed to observe around what is happening to them.

The next day, I unwrapped the tablecloth throughout the table. There was a different letter inside. This time, it was from my mother. I knew it because I could distinguish her penmanship.

This is what my mother's letter says, "I do not tolerate such kind of jokes. If you do that again, you'll sleep outside the mosquito net for a month. Remember that!"

I chuckled from what I read. I pretended that I don't know anything about their letters. I love their act. Their argument was so silent and so unnoticeable.

Another day came, I saw them upon waking---they're having their coffee outside, on the table that is beside the loom. They look good together.

Because of my mischievous nature, I wrote, "Congratulations" then put it under their letters that were hidden within the tablecloth.

I was called for a conversation with them when they noticed my letter. Father gave me a penny to buy ice candy. Then, he told me to stay quiet. I already knew what he wants to say.

I often smile whenever I see a woven table cloth. It is because of that table cloth which had seen the way how father captivates our mother's heart. That table cloth is the witness of their love story.

I also tried that once to my wife when we had a misunderstanding but she just laughed at me. Maybe, that was only effective to my parents because to us, it wasn't.

Face mask- an *abel-iloko* product of Paoay

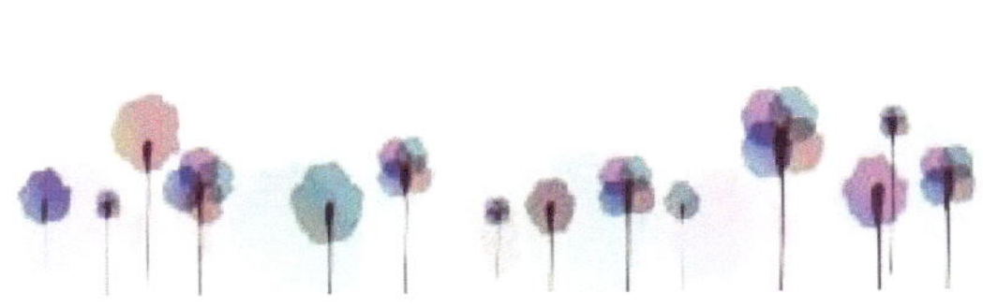

Chapter 2

PAOAY

PAOAY

PAOAY CHURCH : A Grand Cultural Edifice

"The greatness of the things that are beautiful should not perish," I quote. This resembles the beauty and gladness of things to human perception.

Just like Paoay Church, it has a scenic view that most people visit from other parts of the municipality as well as tourists from other countries.

The construction of the Paoay Church started on the year 1953 but was only completed in the year 1964. Some part of the church was

destroyed due to strong earthquakes during the year 1865 and 1885. The last era it was rebuilt was when the time Imelda Marcos became the first lady of the Philippines.

The architectural design was different. Because Paoay Church was the main patron of the Spanish Colonial Baroque who stayed strong till the present days.

The Paoay Church gives a huge impact and lesson to the people who saw it and knew the current situation. It is not only because it was built religiously for Catholics in the Philippines but all Christians.

The Paoay Church is a symbol of resiliency and a great foundation. It was destroyed by an earthquake yet strongly standing. We should be what this church is, that through hard times and challenges that come to us, we should not be torn easily because we have God who can fix the way we live. We should always keep our faith in Him.

I am not a Catholic but I am a Christian who cares for our town. If some friends and relatives came from other places, most especially when they are from afar, I always try to accompany and show them the Paoay Church. One thing that they were really amazed at was the 1.67-meter thickness of the 24 buttresses on the side and back portion of the Church. They say that it was just like a stairway to the top of the building and on heaven.

I thought to myself that we can also strengthen ourselves, we can stay strong always, and we can commit that strength to God.

The tower of the Paoay Church was built beside it. It also lasts for hundreds of years. We should also be like this tower, we should not fall from any hardship, test, troubles, and pain in life. We should not give up yelling and ringing the bell to remind its people about the message of God. Yes, we are also considered as instruments to awaken or to remind people to worship the Almighty.

According to data, approximately five thousand tourists, (local and international) every month visits the Paoay Church. This shows the realistic and main reason why *Paoayeños* and Ilocanos as a whole in the northern part of Luzon should be proud of.

The Paoay Church secretly reminds me to always stand strong. I know that I will not be ruined and destroyed as I am, as long as I care for myself and as long as I have God who molded and created me from dust.

A GREAT CULTURAL CELEBRATION

"A festive gathering brings an exceptional strength."

This maxim is what I often hear from my late grandfather, the reason perhaps is because it displays the spirit of *Guling-guling.*

Guling-guling comes from the *ilokano* word meaning to mark, smear or make a sign. In the olden days, the chieftain (now mayor) of the town would imprint the sign of the cross on a person's forehead using wet, white rice flour. The color

white was significant for it meant purity. Through this marking, a person was thought to be cleansed of all his past sins. Our family would usually join *Guling-guling* because they considered it bad luck to not have markings of it.

There are three remarkable things during *Guling-guling* festival that we need to note: the folk dances, the *Dudol,* and the *Basi.*

First, the folk dances. I could still remember are the *Sabunganay, Paoayena, Ariquen-quen, Curatsa* but I only performed *Sabunganay.* I danced with them because of the belief that this is a meant of forgiving to whom I have had petty squabbles. I also experienced joining an occupational dance, *the agab-abel.* This dance indicates the industriousness and thriftiness of the people.

Second, the *Dudol.* The *dudol* is a native delicacy made from rice flour *(bellaay*), coconut milk (*getta*), sugarcane juice, and anis. During Guling-guling Festival, *dudol* is shared with family friends, and all the guests. My family is fond of making and sharing *dudo*l. 'The act of sharing is a blessing' my mother said. Paoayenos, too, are generous in sharing foods as a symbol of thanksgiving for every fruitful harvest.

Lastly, the *Basi*. *Basi* comes from sugarcane extract and *samak-a* plant commonly grown in Ilocos region. It is the official drink of the *Guling-guling* merrymakers because of its enervating effect. I like *basi,* too, but I prefer the sweetened one.

Being an active participant of this festival, not only the festive nature of the place is seen but it also proves the richness of the culture or the traditions we celebrate.

Neighboring cities also pay a visit during the *Guling-guling* festival. This is one of Paoayenos pride that unites us. I am witness to how Paoay grows. And because of the annual competitions held during the *Guling-guling* festival, dances become lovelier, *Dudol* becomes tastier, meanwhile, *Basi* becomes more spirited. And I believe that there are still more new ideas that our very own people may discover that would add value to our celebrated tradition.

THE CORNICK PRODUCTION OF PAOAY

"There's no harm in trying."

I often read and hear this maxim. Indeed, there is nothing to fear as we try to unlock new things if we firmly trust ourselves without a doubt.

One of whom successfully unlocked things while trying is Mrs. Rosalinda B. Abrogena, also called "Manang Rosa" to those who already knew her. At 60, her Cornick business production has been so productive here at Brgy Sabang, Paoay, Ilocos Norte.

Manang Rosa started a stall of "Binatog", a boiled sweetened corn till she tried to make golden brown crispy corn with her son.

They only hired two workers where they commenced their business. Because her husband is a farmer and has hectares of land that grows corn as a crop, they used their crop as inputs to their production.

Manang Rosa's Cornick was so delicious. And it was visited by near and far-flung cities till their product was traded at Ilocos Sur, Pangasinan, Baguio City then to Metro Manila.

Local tourists love and can't resist coming to her store to buy some. "Only in Paoay" exclaimed those who really enjoyed the unique taste and texture of such product.

Because the business was growing fast, they've added 15 large pans and had to increase their workers.

The business was recognized and hailed by the Small and Medium Enterprise (SME) because of its smooth and quality services.

I honestly believe that even on delicacies of the food industry, Paoay also has something to be known for. This is proof that small dreams can really be fruitful and meaningful.

As usual townsfolk, I also have a plan to put up a business soon upon retiring from teaching. For I firmly believe that like Manang Rosa, I also have the chance and opportunity to succeed.

Indeed, there is also a blessing in trying.

Dudol Making

SYNERGY AND THE "DADAPILAN"

'There is power in helping one another. This simple saying reminds me how important neighborhood is especially during *pinagdadapil* here in Ilocos region.

Every summer reminds me of *Pinagdapil*. It's around November and December where farmers start harvesting their sugarcane and initially do the *dapil*.

There's a lot of products produced by *dapil*. All of them are my favorites. And the municipality of Paoay is known for the sweet delicacies. One of my relatives in this town said: "Our molasses is the

finest. That is why it is marketable. Besides, we mold them in different sizes."

Panagdapil is the process of extracting sugar cane juice from its pulp using a conventional or a modern machine. The use of a traditional type of *dapil* is getting rare nowadays since modern machines are much more convenient. With the old type, they employ the service of the carabao to pull the wooden *dapil* to rotate clockwise while the farmer is busy inserting the sugar cane stems to be pressed. The juice flows down as they collect it into a big pot or *siliasi* or *sinublan*. If they have collected enough then they heat it through the fire. The heat varies depending on what product you want to achieve. Slight heating is necessary for making *basi* or wine followed by *suka* or vinegar. Further heating is required to turn it into molasses ready for *kalti*. It's a way to dip papaya strips, *malagkit* to make *kaskaron* for snacks. *Silamot* is a term used to pinch the cooled molasses and eat it. Everyone in the neighborhood helps to make this happens and party over the *kalti* and *silamot*.

I like the sweetness of the sugarcane's sucrose called '*bennal*' while other residents called it '*palutipot*'. This sweet thing tells about Paoayenos of being sweet, grateful, affectionate, and gentle, too. In addition to, molasses, wine, and vinegar as a finished product from sugar cane is clean and pure.

One lesson I learned during *panagdapi*l is the need for enough patience in doing the best outcome of what we desire.

While writing this, I plan to take a picture of *Dadapilan*, a wooden sugar mill. How I wish the municipality will uphold and conserve this traditional *Dadapilan* for small molasses producers.

AS CONFIDENT AS A SAND DUNES

I always remember what an anonymous poet once said, that we are collected sand washed by time and sea waves. And I found myself just a tiny particle in the universe.

When I was a child, I usually used to play at Paoay sand dunes. It is my favorite playground. According to my parents, they buried my feet between the wet and dry sands near the seashore when I started to stand and pace a new step. This is a belief that a baby could walk easier if it is done so.

The Paoay sand dune is about an 8-square kilometer parched paradise that lies adjacent to Suba Beach in Paoay, Ilocos Norte. It has been opened for sand boarding and four-wheel riding the 4X4 extreme adventure. The place is also one of the local and even a national favorite when it comes to filming. This is also considered a historical and cultural landmark of the municipality.

I had unforgettable memories in this place. It happened when I was emotionally sick. I went alone to this sand dunes, sat on its peak, and upon in deep meditation everything in this scene was graceful, beautiful, and conducive to serenity. Its benign peacefulness laid healing, quieting touch upon me. I closed my eyes and I realized I am compared to sand- small, tiny yet beautiful. Sometimes amid active and busy lives, I have found the dunes profitable to see and stop for a minute or two to experience once again the remarkable power to quiet, to soothe, and to relax in the beauty of nature. Since then, I have considered Paoay Sand Dunes as one of the most beautiful and relaxing scenes I've ever seen. It may have slight changes due to natural challenges but its beauty is unchanged.

The lesson is, though how tiny we are if we stand together as one, we become stronger and more beautiful. Never underestimate our worth. We are sand. We are great. We are beautiful.

LESSONS FROM THE SAND DUNES

I remember a famous quotation from American writer Robert M. Pirsig and I quote: "We take a handful of sand from the endless landscape of awareness around us and call that handful of sand the world."

This quotation now reminds me of how beautiful the Paoay Sand Dunes is and gives me a flashback of my childhood memories. It brings me back to the good old times when I used to grasp sands using my tiny hands. It gives me time to

introspect and reminisce the tiny lessons I learned from the dunes.

The Paoay Sand Dunes is an 88- square kilometer parched paradise that lies adjacent to Suba Beach in Paoay, Ilocos Norte. It is now a popular site for sandboarding, 4x4 vehicle riding, and filming. But what others do not know about it is that it actually has been my source of wisdom and inspiration as I traversed life. Aside from it is both a historical and cultural landmark of the municipality, it has beautiful lessons to share. The profundity of the life lessons it reflects will surely lead someone to greater heights.

Three great lessons had been imprinted in my heart. These lessons are not footprints in the sand, rather, I call them the footprints in my heart. Whenever I have a glance at the Paoay Sand Dunes, I really can't stop my tears to fall.

The first lesson that the Paoay Sand Dunes had taught me is the value of flexibility. The Paoay Sand Dunes changes from time to time according to wind direction and weather. Thus, it taught me the importance of adjusting yourself in any situation. You must know how to blend with the current situation and to dance with the wind. Whatever the weather is, the sand dunes were able to withstand all the natural challenges that tested their strength and were able to preserve their beauty.

The second lesson I learned is the value of self-confidence. Even though how tiny grain of sand is, it was the reason why the Paoay Sand Dunes exists. Like a tiny grain of sand, we are also tiny elements that make the universe complete. Thus, even though how little you think of yourself, always keep that confidence in you. Maybe if I didn't have that confidence, I might have not written this book. I may not be as prolific as other writers are, but my confidence led me to my dream of becoming a book author. Never underestimate yourself because you, too, can do great things. Wear that confidence and go for your dreams!

Lastly, the third golden lesson from the sand dunes is the value of self-contentment. When I was a child, I used to build sandcastles. However, these sandcastles end up to nothing. All beautiful things end up to nothing unexpectedly. Thus, self-contentment should always be a virtue to uphold. Always learn to appreciate the small things that you have. Indeed, these lessons are life-changing. Always inculcate them in your heart and mind so that you may use them as powerful weapons in your battlefield called life.

TUMBA-TUMBA: SCARY YET REMARKABLE

"Flesh and bone might soon be banished, but the good memories it left remain forever," my best friend once told us on our loved ones that were long gone. This is also the reason why the Municipality of Paoay, Ilocos Norte, celebrates the *Tumba-Tumba* festival to commemorate the memories of our dead.

The *Tumba-Tumba* Festival is the highlight of the provincial Halloween event of Ilocos Norte. It is also called the 'Semana ti Ar-aria (ghost week)

which runs from October 27 to November 3. This festival is a form of atonement for the spirit of the dead which are believed are not yet raised to God or still imprisoned at the purgatory. Until it became a town competition because it was seen by the municipality of Paoay that it has potential in tourism and how various communities converge for the event.

During the *Tumba-tumba* Festival, we always help in constructing huts. Each hut represents a cluster of Barangays. Inside each hut is a *tumba* (catafalque) laden with offerings for the dead which usually include cigarettes, betel nuts, busi, wine rice and *atang* - ilocano indigenous snacks to be served to the visitors.

I once tried the participation of dung-aw (mourning cry). We usually wear 'baro't saya', especially made from 'inabel', an ilokano blouse and skirt ensemble.

I tried to participate in this activity. Our barangay also had the chance to bring home runners up award. We could notice here how well organized and unified the townsfolk are.

Every *Tumba-tumba* festival, we fervently celebrates because, along the entire Luzon, it is only in Paoay where we could witness such tradition of mourning. For others, it is frightening but for us, we consider it as a distinct art of praying and raising the spirits to God or commemorating the dead ones.

I could say that this old tradition is one of which makes Paoay was known. And Paoay will be remembered in this traditional event of the North. It's the only festival with artistic *atang* nationally and internationally displayed as well.

THE AMAZING MIGRATORY BIRDS OF NAGBACALAN

"I take pride in my hometown for having such a healthy and grandeur lake. Its beauty and cleanliness have been preserved for our next generation to see and enjoy," Rod Sadian, a bird watcher enthusiast of Paoay said.

The 387-hectare Paoay Lake National Protected Landscape is the feeding point of migratory birds.

We, the locals of Paoay, Ilocos Norte are the most excited of all, as flocks of different bird

species from neighbouring countries naturally migrate to our town.

Since the first holding of the Festival 2008, local birders have frequented the lake's view deck in Nagbacalan Village for a chance to see migratory birds.

Years ago, bird watching has slowly gained popularity enticing local and foreign enthusiasts using binoculars, telescopes, and high-end cameras. Paoay Lake is considered one of the country's important migratory bird sites.

Based on the latest Asian Waterbird Census, the Philippines duck is commonly seen in the area with an average of 600 while Little Grebe, Great Egret, Little Egret, Cattle Egret, Tufted Duck, White brow Crane, Common Kingfisher, White Collared Kingfisher, White Throat Kingfisher and the Cormorant (which is almost everyone's favourite) are commonly seen in the Lake.

We people migrate, too. We look and search a place to rove and wander.

If the lake has different birds to live (be it temporary or not), the municipality of Paoay has different Pilipino races with different languages, too. We all live in a community where love and peace reign.

I often call the attention of some of my friends and relatives to visit and see the beauty of Paoay. "Migrate like birds. If birds can, why can't we," I challenge them.

MALACAÑANG OF THE NORTH

"The Malacañang of the North is a presidential museum in Paoay, Ilocos Norte. It was the residence of the family of Ferdinand Marcos when he was the president of the Philippines," Julie Mer Laverinto- Lagui describes.

" I'm impressed! This mansion or Malacañang of the North is well maintained. I suggest having your guide for more engagement with the guests. From there, I love d the Paoay lake view," Lancelot Xjo says.

"The place will give you peek of what was the life back then of the Marcoses. It also offers a view of the lake where some boat racing

competitions were held. This place is mostly used as wedding venues now," Kris Rivera, a local tourist suggests.

A mansion overlooking the sea, Malacañang of the North served as home of former President Ferdinand E. Marcos. Today, it functions as a museum detailing the turbulent political situation when Marcos ruled under Martial Law-- which ended a revolution in 1986.

The mansion consists of seven rooms, with each room having a theme of historical events from the Marcos era: study, agriculture, diplomacy, OFW, culture and nation-building, and family.

The Study Room features extensive book collections, some of which Marcos authored.

The Agriculture Room gives a glimpse of the agriculture programs including the rice production under the Masagana 99 project. That period was the construction of various dams across the country.

The diplomacy room provides a history of Marcos' foreign and international trade relations, primarily with Asian neighbours.

The Nation Building Room describes the rise of infrastructure programs that linked Ilocos Norte to Zamboanga City through bridges and roads. That was when Patapat viaduct in Pagudpud, Ilocos Norte and the San Juanico bridge were built

The OFW Room is a tribute to Ilocano overseas workers who are spread across the globe.

The Culture Room is a preview of the era of the cultural renaissance which former First Lady Imelda Marcos once upheld.

The Family Room shows the former president wearing a different hat, from one who is perceived as untouchable to a simple man.

Today, the mansion is open for everyone. Tour guides on hand can answer all of your questions. If you are there for just the architecture and art, just walk around by yourself and admire numerous paintings on the walls.

Come.

Visit Paoay and let's dig more about the history of the great man thru this great mansion.

CHARITO CARRIAGA, THE LIVING LEGEND OF PAOAY

The vast and rich century-old history may be long gone but the remnants were again made alive that it brings us all back in time.

Ilocano's loom weaving, particularly in the Ilocos region, has gone global reflecting the rich design tradition and rural lifestyle. This is no surprise. Primarily because it has been really part of the tradition of the Ilocandia even since the pre-Spanish era. It has been a growing demand and a major export of the galleon trade probably because the Spaniards really admired not only how intricate the design was but also the durability and superior quality it has showcased. The living witness to such perhaps is the Paoay church which was built during Spanish time as a reward to them for their trade. However, the tradition has been facing a risk of cultural extinction because the interest of the younger generation in loom weaving has been waning. But, fortunately, the loom weaving tradition has found its keepers.

Charito Carriaga, a renowned leader of local weavers at Paoay, Ilocos Norte, believes that the loom-weaving industry should continue to enrich the Ilokano tradition. She also considers it as a bridge to history. Hence, she spearheaded and founded the Nagbacalan Loom Weavers Multi-Purpose Cooperative.

The Cooperative has already made an appearance at a product showcase exhibit with the international community such as the Center for International Trade Expositions and Missions, and this by far their most notable achievement.

But, how did they successfully revive the tradition?

Carriaga took the challenge of the council members to lead the loom weavers of their community because no one dared and willing to become one. They had faced challenges of modernization, lack of raw materials, and scarcity of funds.

With an initial capital of only P 5,300, the group which is then composed of only 13 female weavers, started showcasing to the local and global community their skills that had stunned the world before. From traditional *abel* blankets and pillowcases, they expanded their product range to placemats, table napkins, runners, bags, dress materials, and all kinds of handwoven items.

"Whatever the people want us to make, we produce," Mrs. Carriaga said.

"Other weavers set their prices low to attract more buyers, but our products are more expensive because of the quality of both the craftsmanship and the materials," she further emphasized.

Government assistance played a great role in the development of the cooperative. For instance, the Cooperative Development Authority gave a P 250,000 of financial assistance for their building, meanwhile, the Department of Social Welfare and Development (DSWD) gave an interest-free P 30,000 loan. This was really helpful for the welfare of the members of the cooperative.

Now, the cooperative has grown more members with an asset of around 3 million and plans to expand its horizons, according to Carriaga.

Had it not been because of the initiatives of our visionary leader, and committed members, the century-old tradition that contains imprints of our heritage may have already lost its magnificence in our society today.

What a sight of remorse if our national treasure was lost had it not been because of our dearest Carriaga.

AN ENCOUNTER WITH THE LEGEND, CHARITO CARRIAGA

Without her, we are probably not what we are today.

It was one hot afternoon when I along with a friend had the opportunity to meet the living legend of Paoay, Charito Carriaga. Despite her age, she was still very articulate and responsive in sharing with us how she achieved the challenging task of restoring the century-old tradition of weaving and helping the townsfolks of Paoay.

She was so hesitant before to take the challenge of the barangay council because she had no idea how or where to get materials. Moreover, how will they finance it? But with her husband's consoling advice and support, she accepted the leadership role of the association of local weavers.

Believe it or not, their association led by her which later on became a cooperative only started with 13 members and with a capital of 5,000 pesos that started in 1992. But today, she alone has now 30 *Abel* weavers and the cooperative has an asset running to millions.

Their first *Abel* was so laborious. They would buy cotton from the farmers and naturally dye it to be able to produce their own thread. As the demand goes higher in the market, they decided to buy commercialized threads to sustain the higher needs of their clients. However, the quality created of the finished products justifies the price it was tagged.

Aside from the blankets, towels, and table runners they commonly produce, they also sustain *abel* for the uniforms worn by our dearest teachers including me, and the students' uniforms which are all products of the cooperative including the outfits used in the Guling-Guling Festival. They even make *maong abels* for jeans seen to be worn by common people.

She explained that " If you work with your own hands, the quality is higher, that is the difference from the *Abel* in the commercial market."

Throughout the years, since 1992, the local weavers continuously stun the country through exhibiting their locally made *Abel.* This was because of Charito's firm leadership and untiring effort to introduce the product to different places; may it be on a local or an international level.

The artistry of local weavers could be seen in their unique designs. They often recreate a new design from their old design concepts.

One of their greatest challenges perhaps is the propagation of imitation as it became widespread that it affects the *Abel*-made products. They once saw their own design copied in Marikina where vendors tell their buyers that it was from Paoay. This claim nearly got one of Charito's fellow weavers into a heated argument with a vendor where they went there to sell some authentic *Abel* made from Paoay.

Charito frequently shouldered the expenses of the association, including taxes, as a way to finance it. Because of her promising potential as a public figure, she was asked to run in politics to which she undoubtedly refused.

She also refused her only daughter's request to retire and reside in the US with her four grandchildren for she constantly thinks about the local weavers.

Without the Cooperative, the weavers perhaps won't be able to own land, build a home and send their kids to school, which they did because of Charito's leadership.

I was also a witness to how the cooperative helped my mother in raising us. The cooperative really empowers those who need support the most.

Our dearest Charito Carriaga proves that a clear vision with a passion to lead outweighs the challenges and for this very reason, I know and I'm certain, ----- people will pay her good deeds a thousand folds.

ABOUT THE AUTHOR

JENIFER CRACAR-MACADANGDANG

Jenifer Cracar-Macadangdang was born on January 18, 1978 at Paoay, Ilocos Norte. The second eldest daughter of the late Mr. Simplicio Galano Caracar and the loom weaver Mrs. Ofelia Lumang Bautista.

She is married to Mr. Rufino O. Macadangdang, Jr and blessed with two lovely and God-fearing daughters namely Kyle Zyrah and Ana Carmella.

Jenifer finished her primary education at Nagbacalan Elementary School in 1991, her secondary education at Paoay Lake National High School in 1995, and finished her College education at the one of the prestigious school in the Philippines, the Mariano Marcos State University – College of Education Laoag City with the Degree bachelor of Elementary Education and graduated in 1999.

Her education never stops. She took her Master's Degree at Mariano Marcos State University Graduate School Laoag City major in MAPEH and Guidance and Counseling as her Cognate. Her thirst to professional growth continued in St. Mary's Academy, Sta. Maria Ilocos Sur took up Master of Arts in Education major in Administration and Supervision.

After her graduation in 1999, she immediately applied as preschool teacher at Faith Preschool, Inc. Now the Paoay Faith Academy Inc. In 1999-2001. Her successful journey continues at Dingras Faith Academy Inc. Dingras, Ilocos Norte in 2001-2002. And in 2002-2004 at Merry Mount Preparatory School of Quezon City and designated as the Teacher-In-Charge.

Her determination, devotion and commitment to teaching leads her to a greater heights. Last February 27, 2004, the door to public service widely opened for her. She was appointed as Teacher I at Nagbacalan West Primary School now Nagbacalan West Elementary School and luckily assigned as Teacher-In-Charge for 6 years. Promoted Teacher II in 2006.

At present, she is a dedicated Public School Teacher II at Nagbacalan Elementary School, designated Information Communication Technology (ICT) Coordinator and the Guidance Coordinator of the same school since her transfer in 2017.

Aside from training achievements she attended that made her who she is today, she is a proud Paoayeño and that encouraged her to write this book, PANGABLAN: THE LIVING

TREASURE OF PAOAY" which personally dedicated to her family, to her mother Ofelia and to her beloved town – Paoay.

www.ingramcontent.com/pod-product-compliance
Ingram Content Group UK Ltd.
Pitfield, Milton Keynes, MK11 3LW, UK
UKHW060358300726
14090UKWH00001B/15

9786218261501